Stress Reliever

Take a Breather and COLOR!

by Lisa Bengtson

Take a Breather and COLOR!

The new wave of stress release is Coloring.
Everyone handles stress differently.
How you color to release your stress is up to you.
You know your body and mind. Some need to absentmindedly color.
Others use one or two colors only. While some use every color they
have in their collection. You Decide...

* Choose a pattern;
* If you feel pressured for time, set your timer so you can relax and
not worry while coloring;
* Breathe in and out calmly;
* Let your mind rest so new ideas and/or solutions will come to you;
* Find peace and relaxation in your breathing and coloring;
* If you feel your tension rise or your body gets stiff, take a moment
to breathe in and out calmly and then resume your coloring.
* When you are ready to stop coloring, stop. Resume or start a new
pattern the next time.
* Don't feel pressured to finish the design you're coloring.
This will defeat you in your quest. Remember, you can always
resume later. Then only do what relieves the stress.

Let Go and Relax.
Be More Productive in Everything You Do
because You Took a Breather and Colored!

Make Your Life Richer through Relaxation Coloring!

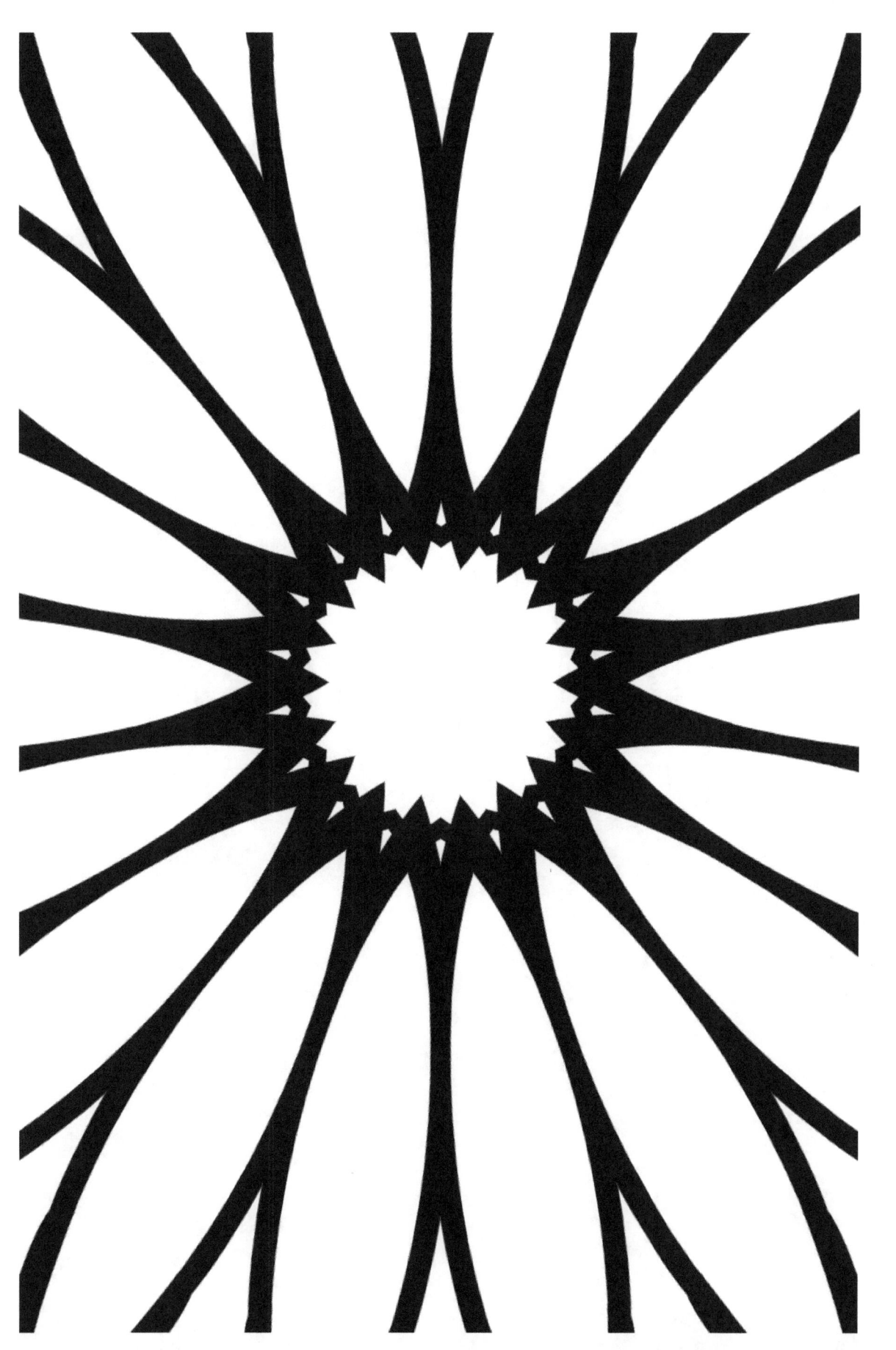

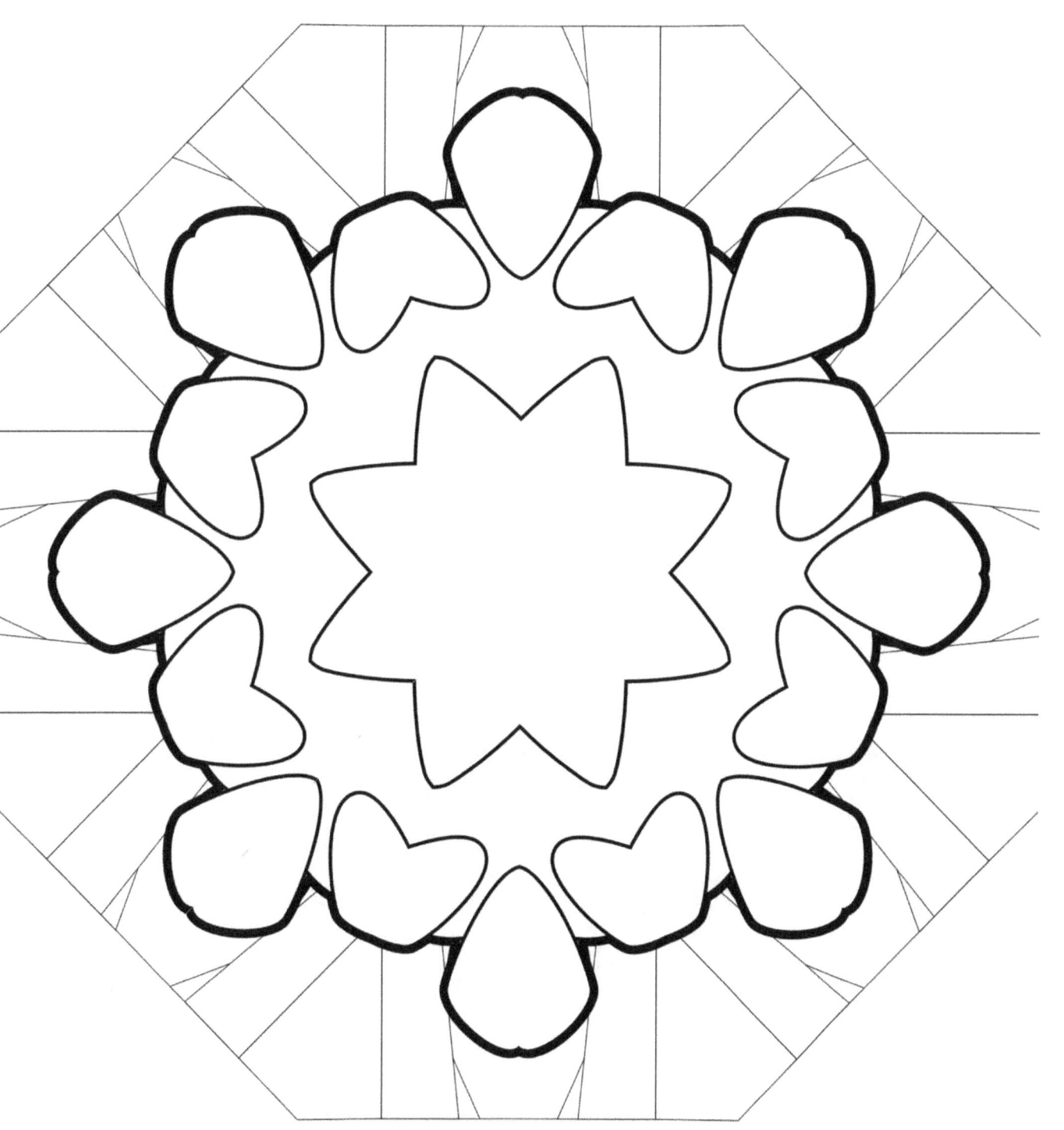

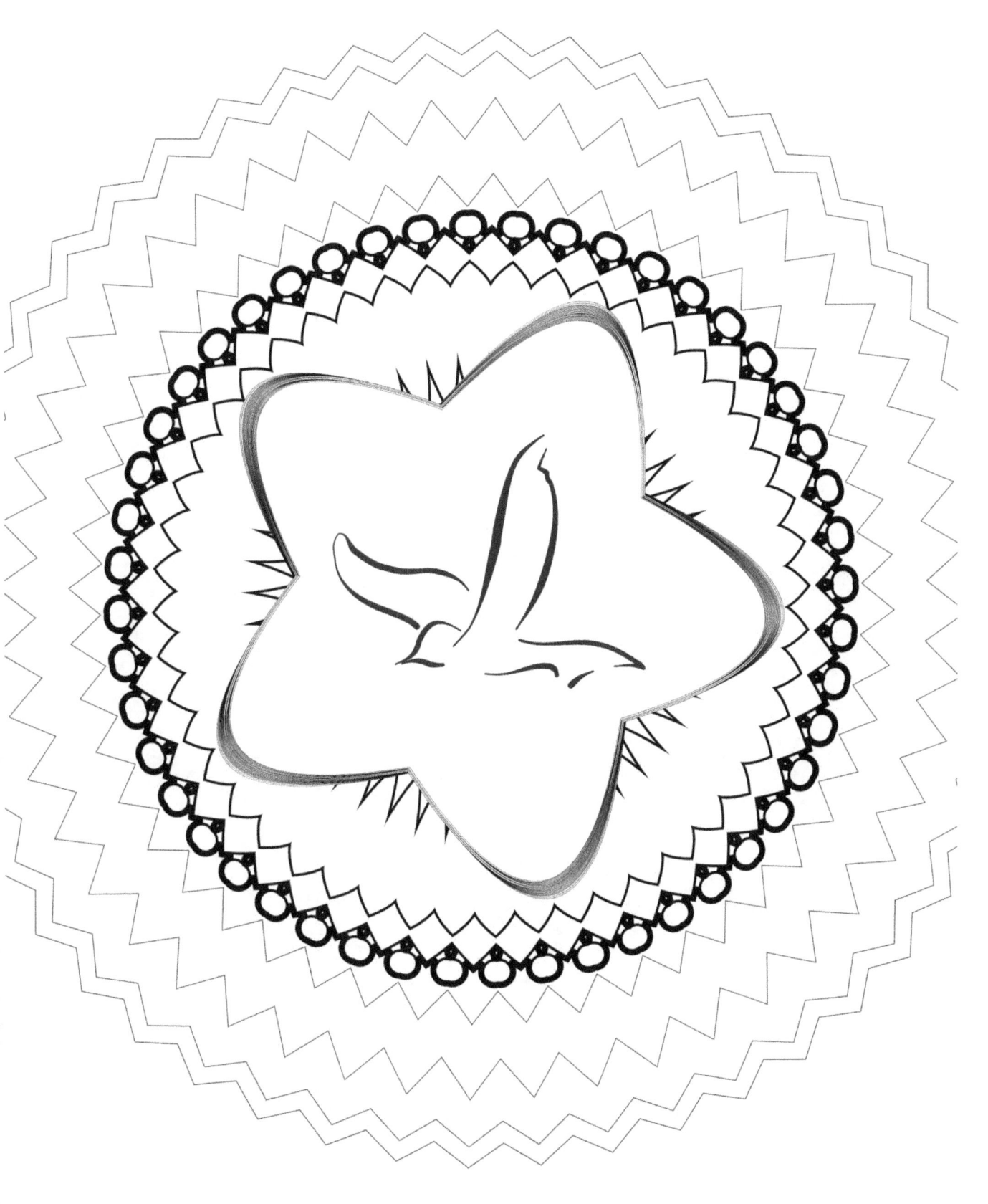

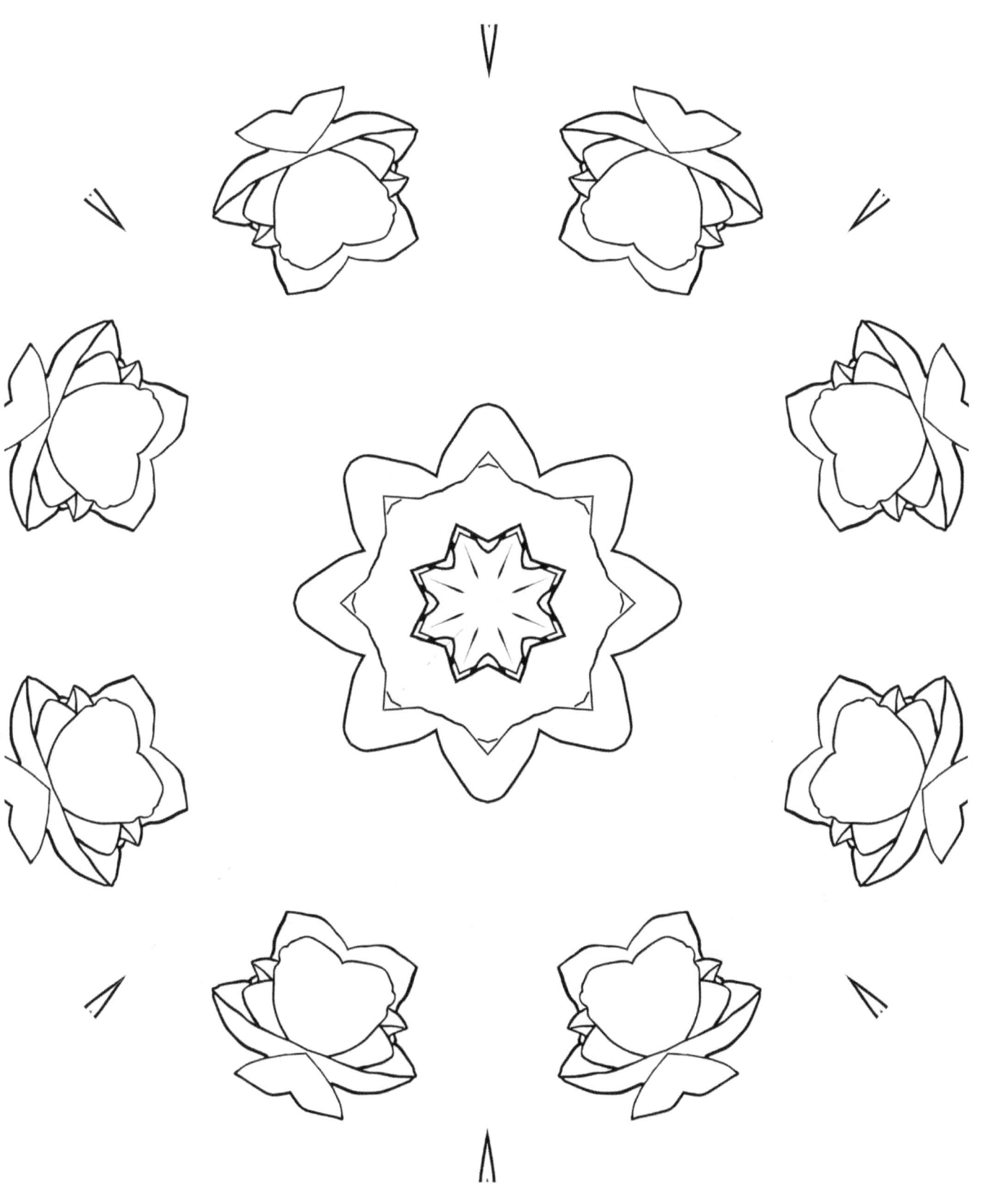

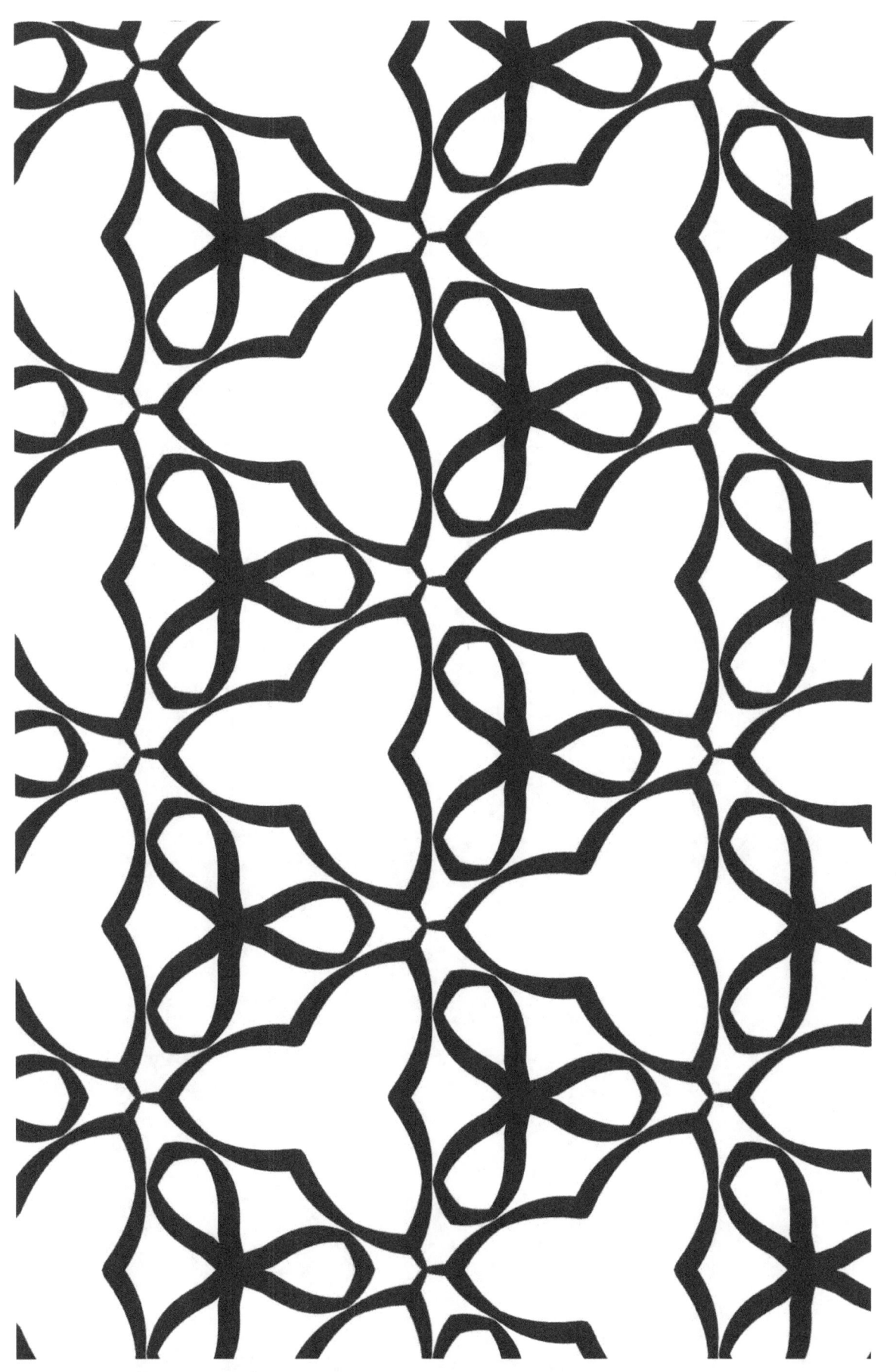

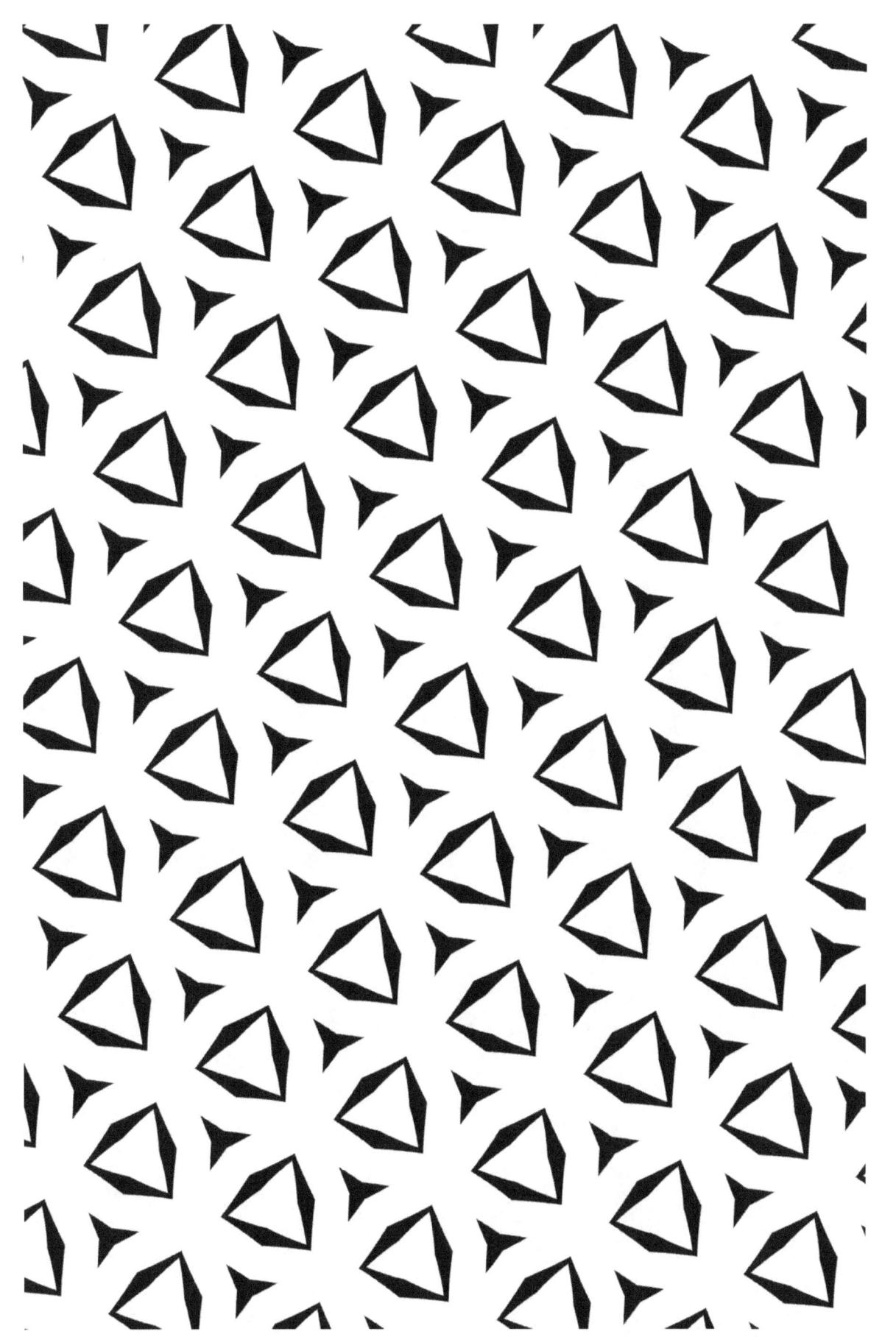

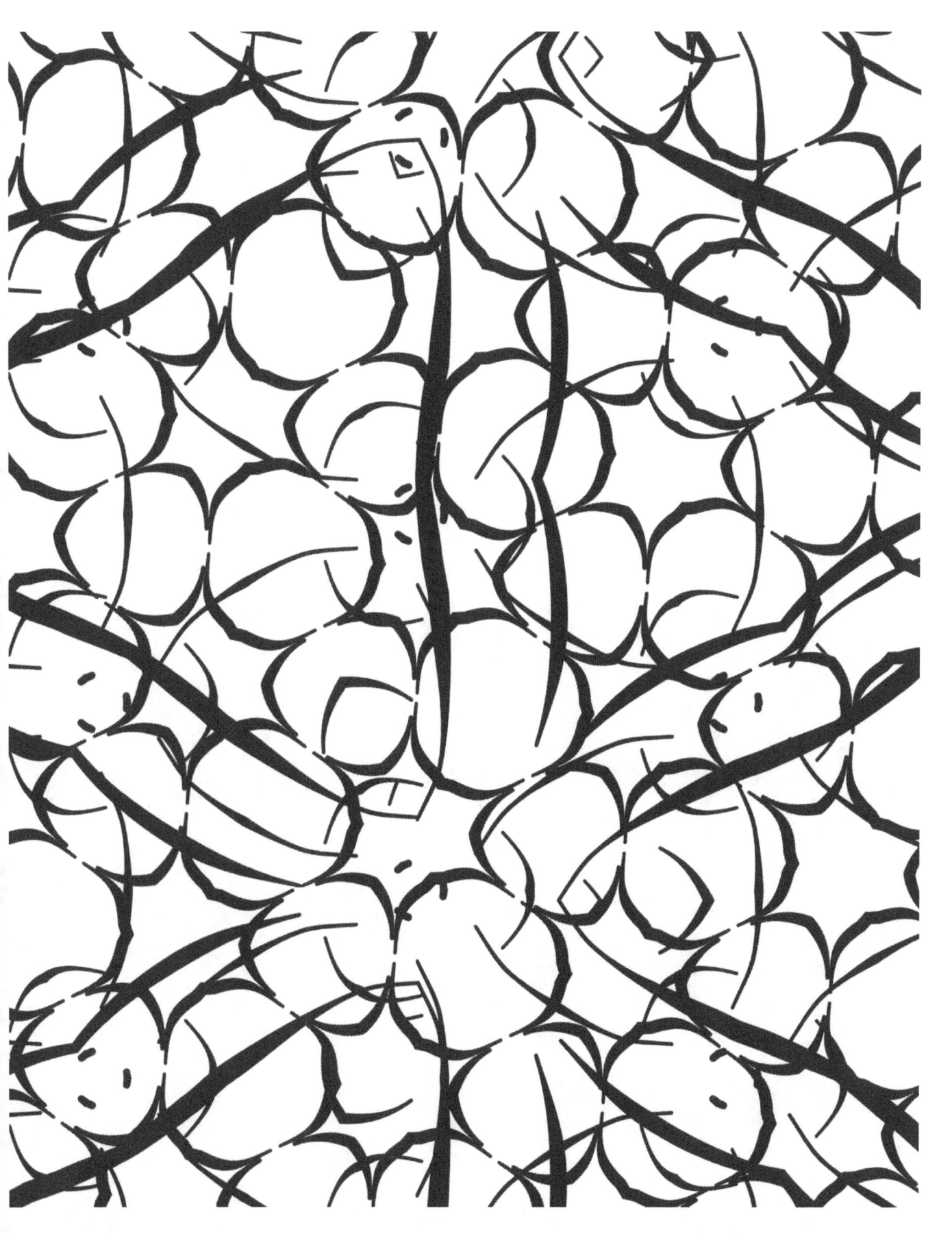

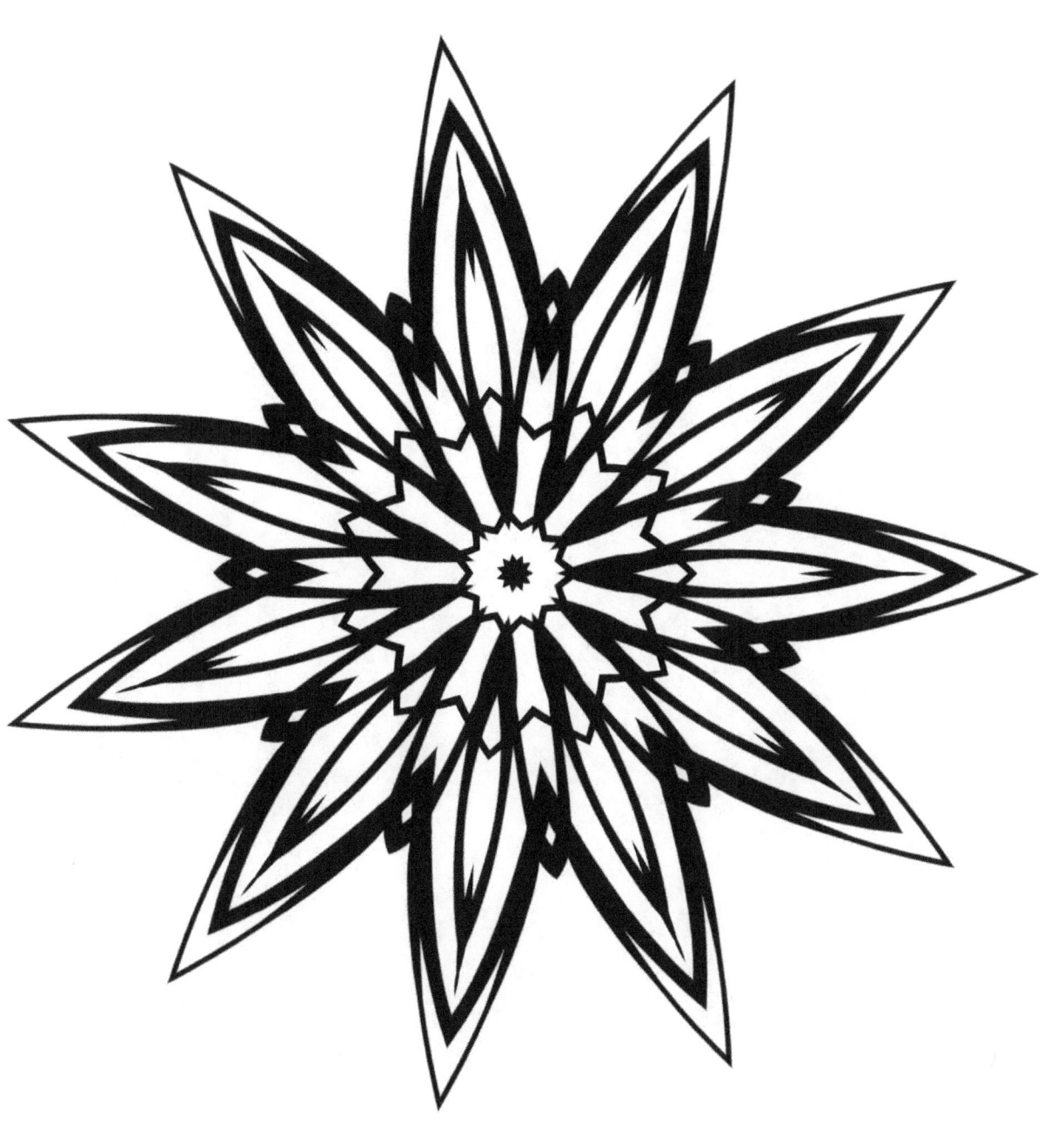

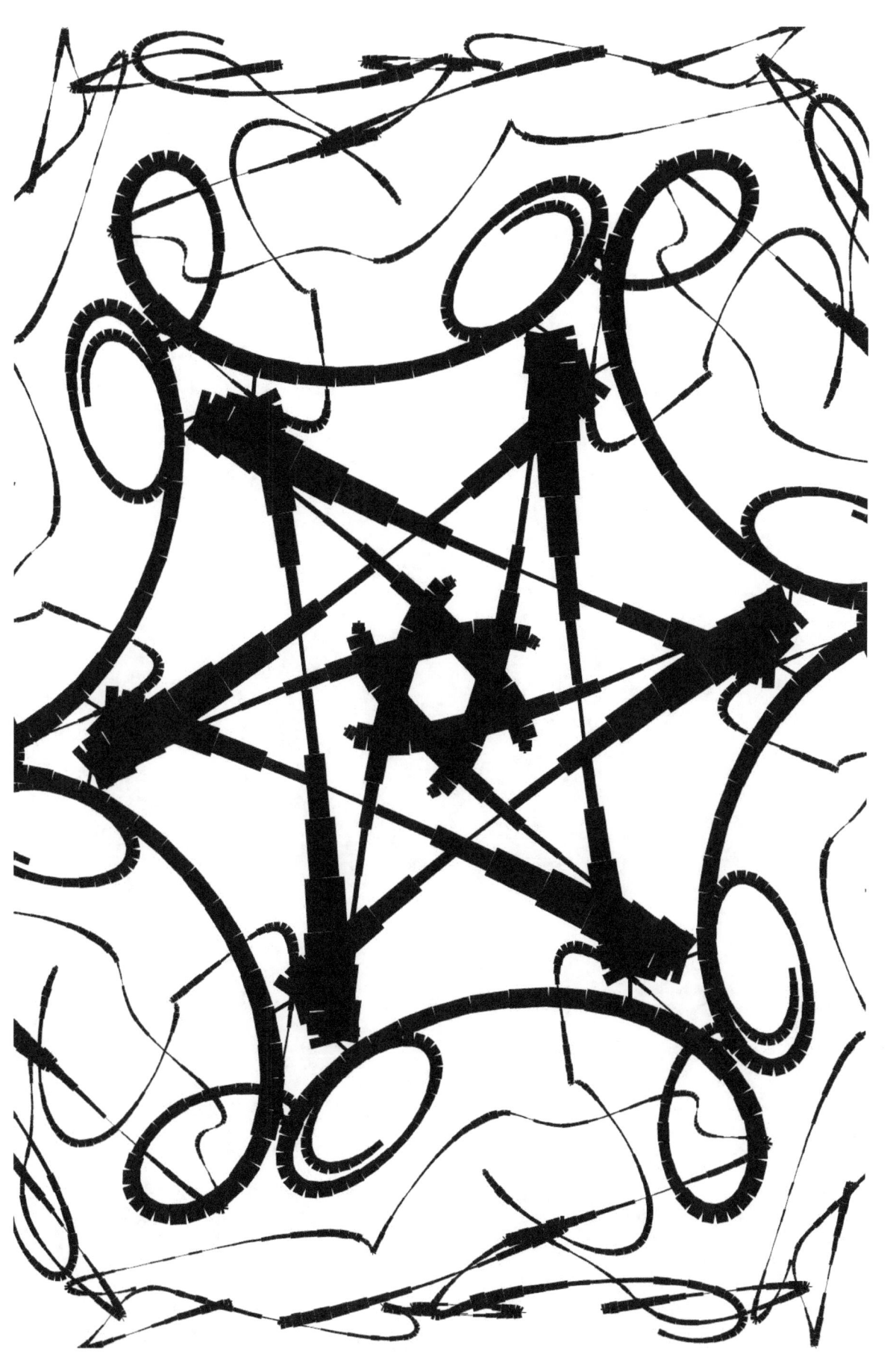

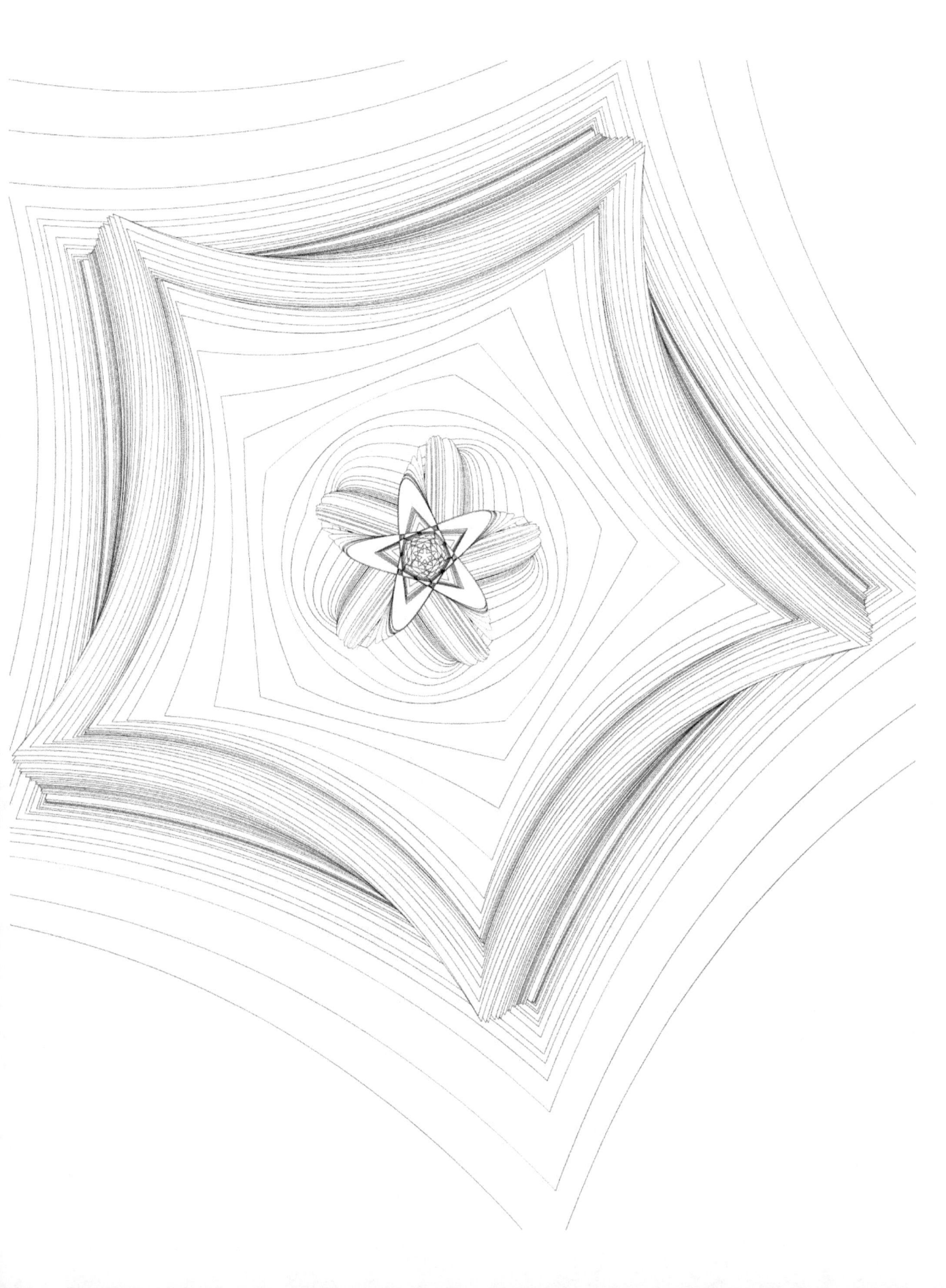

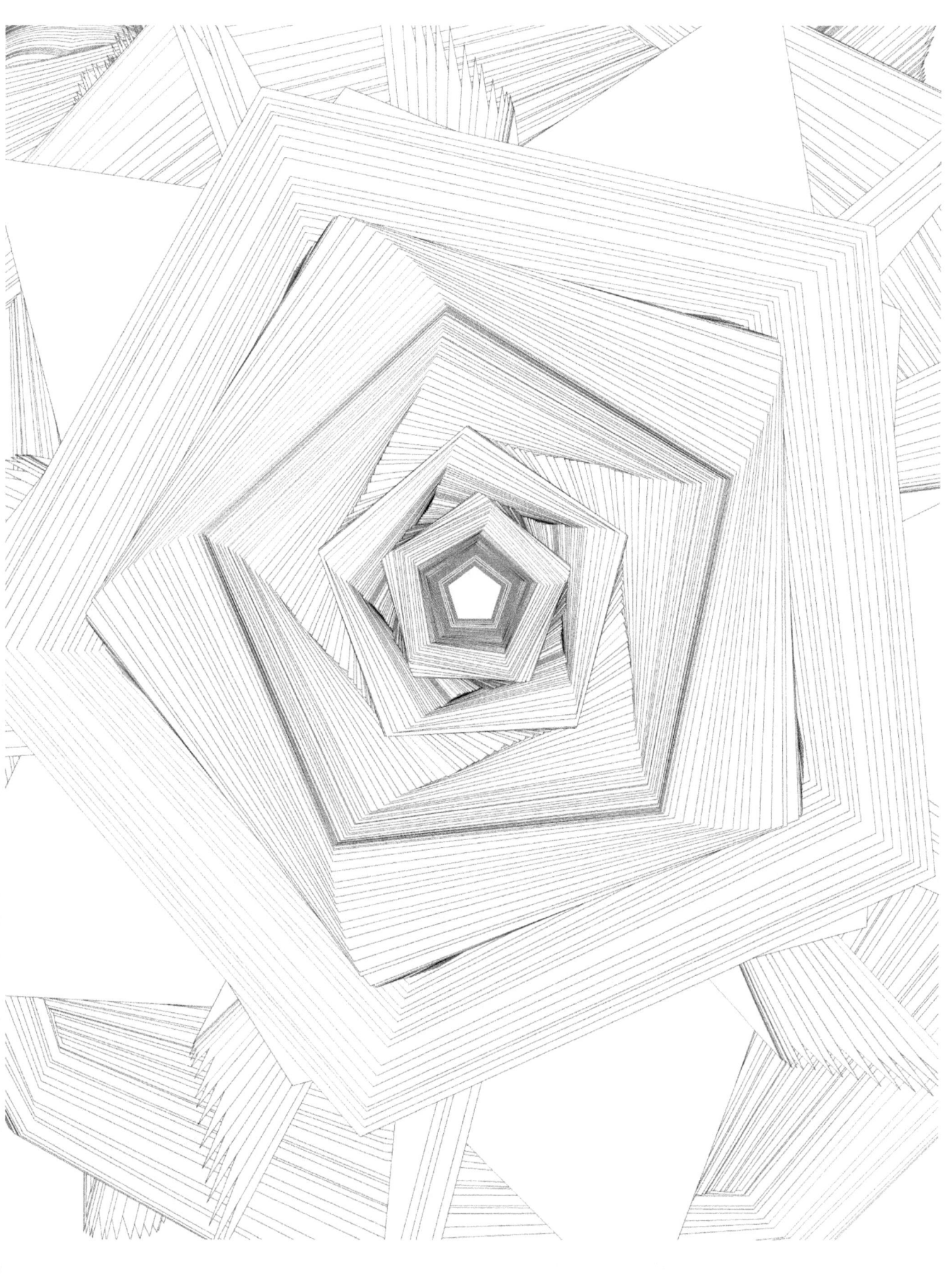

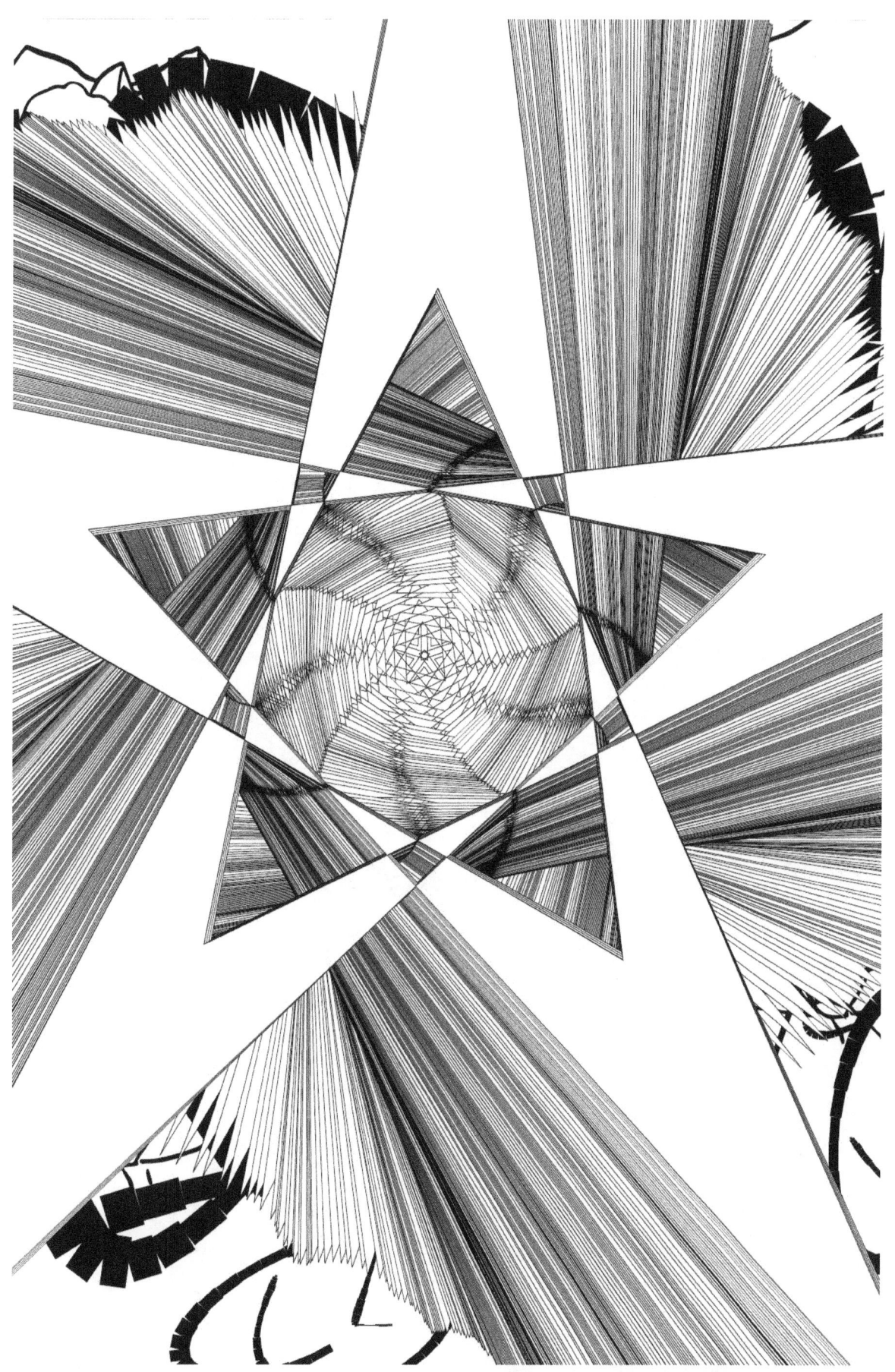

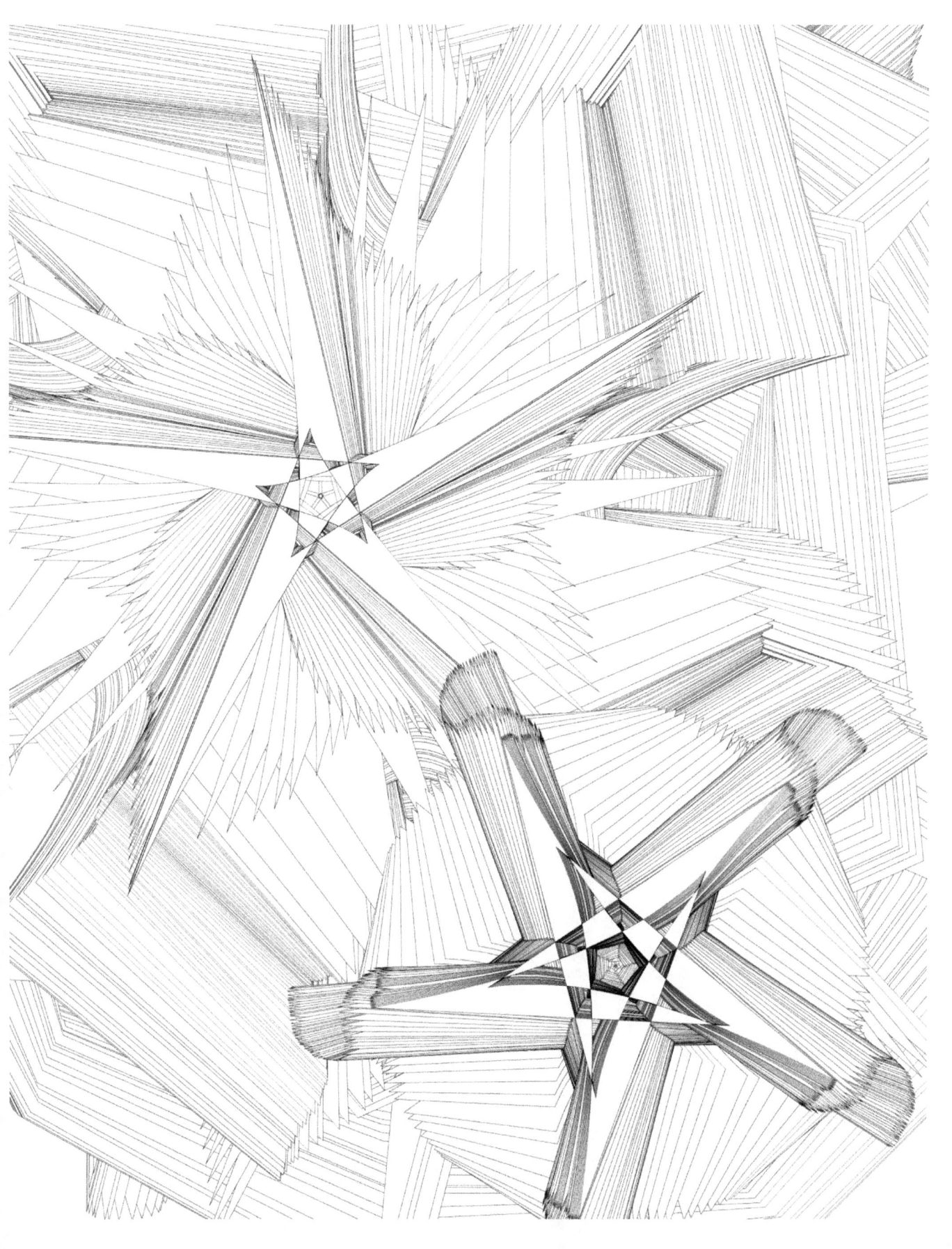

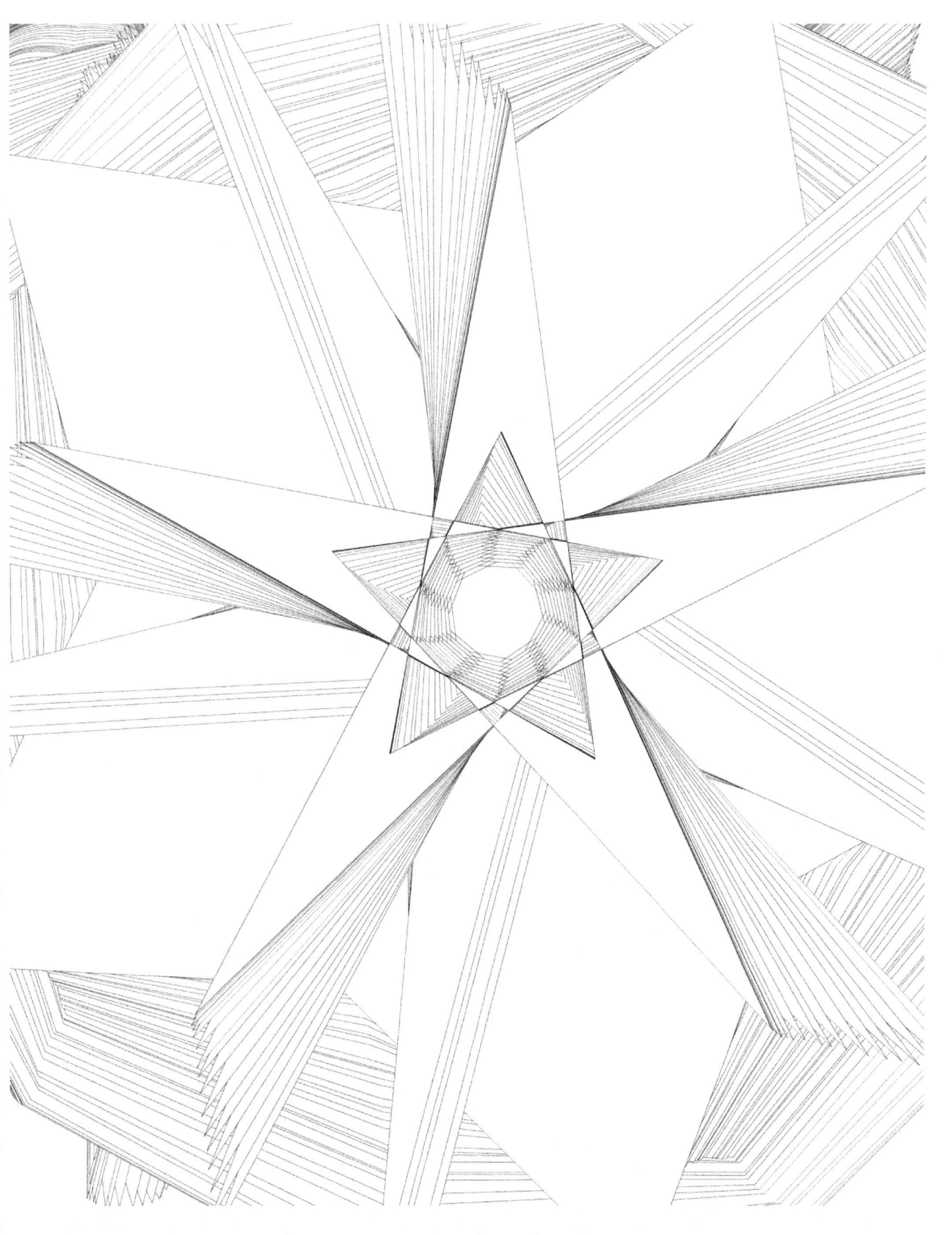

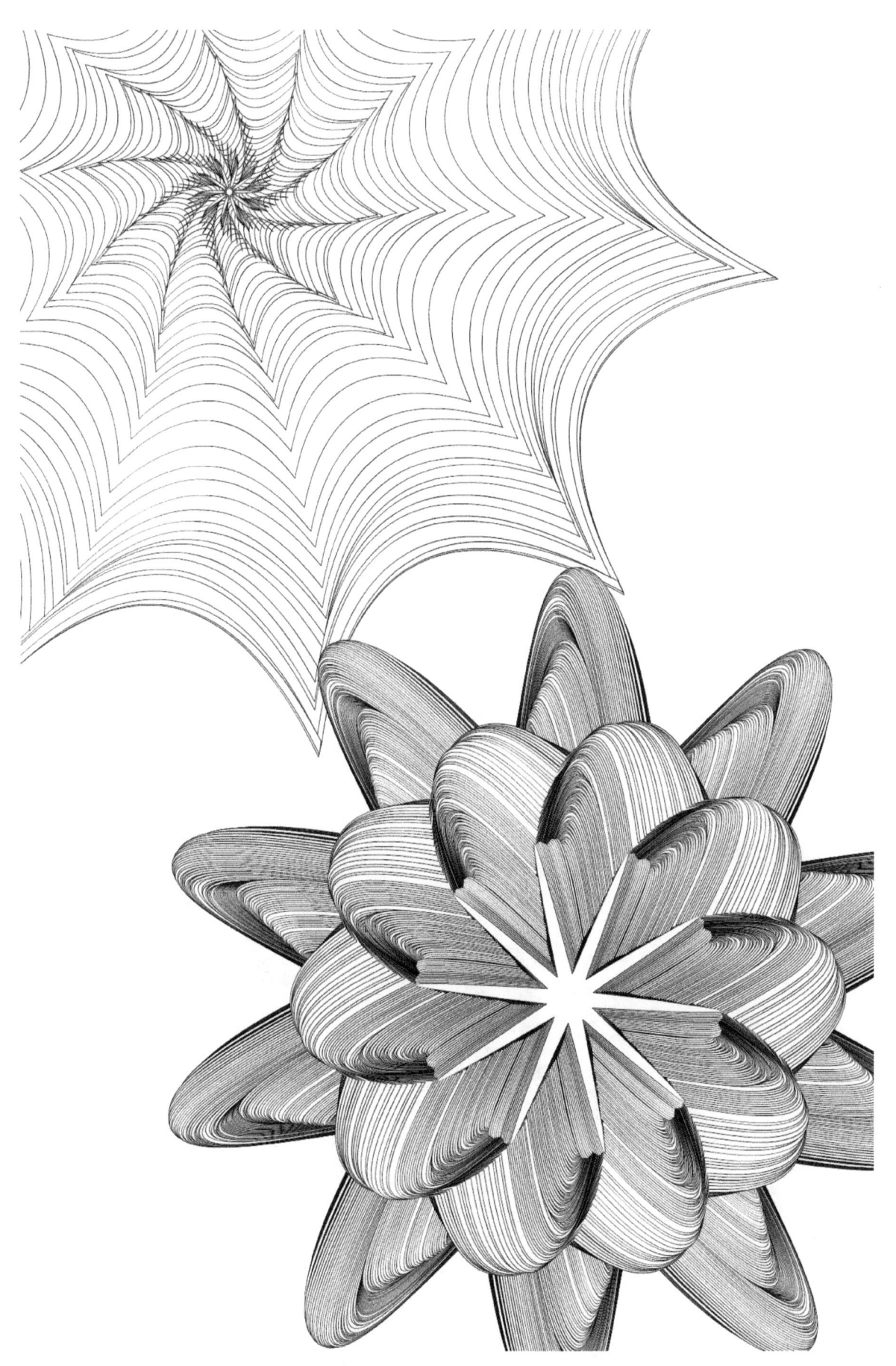

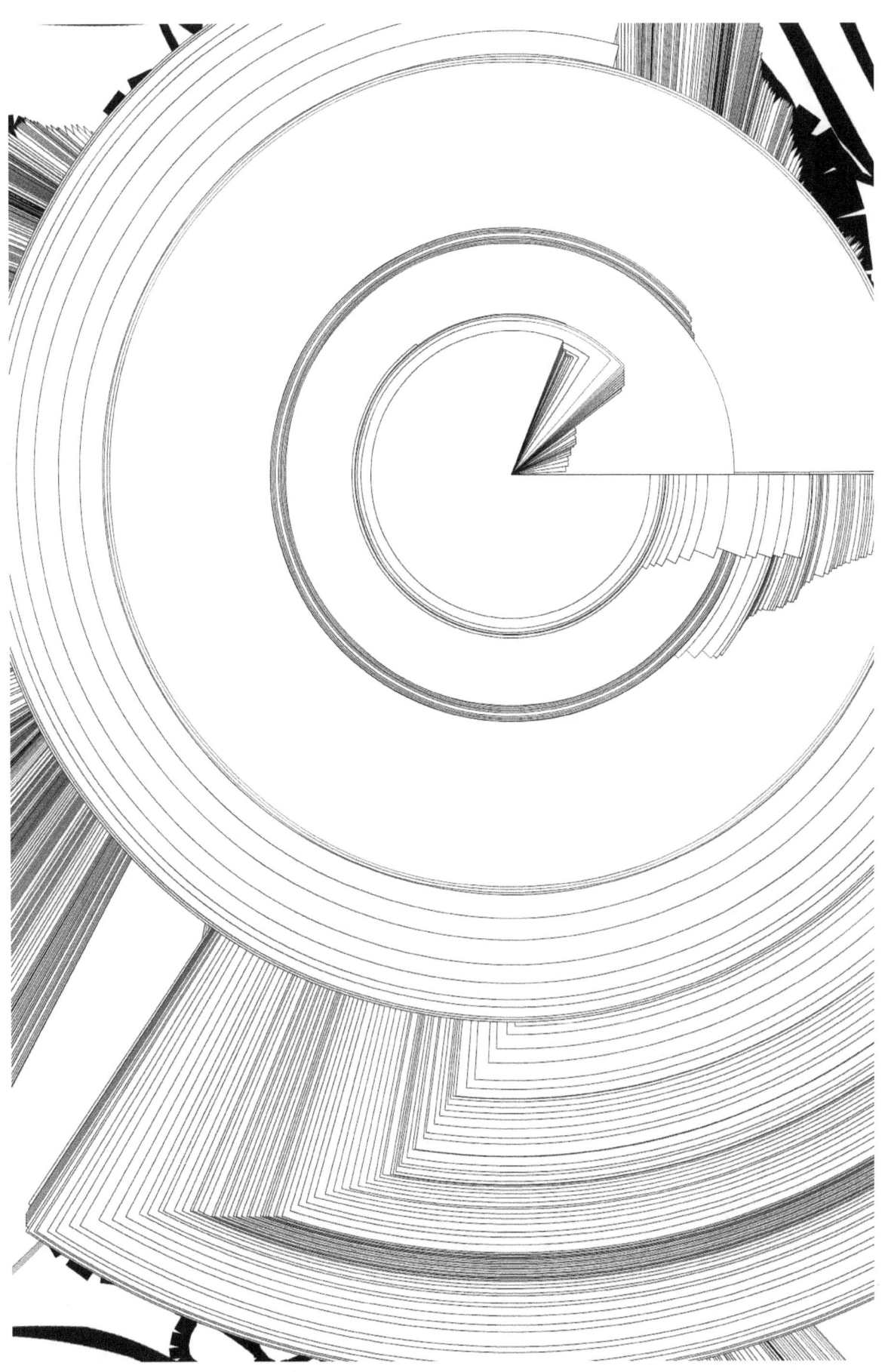

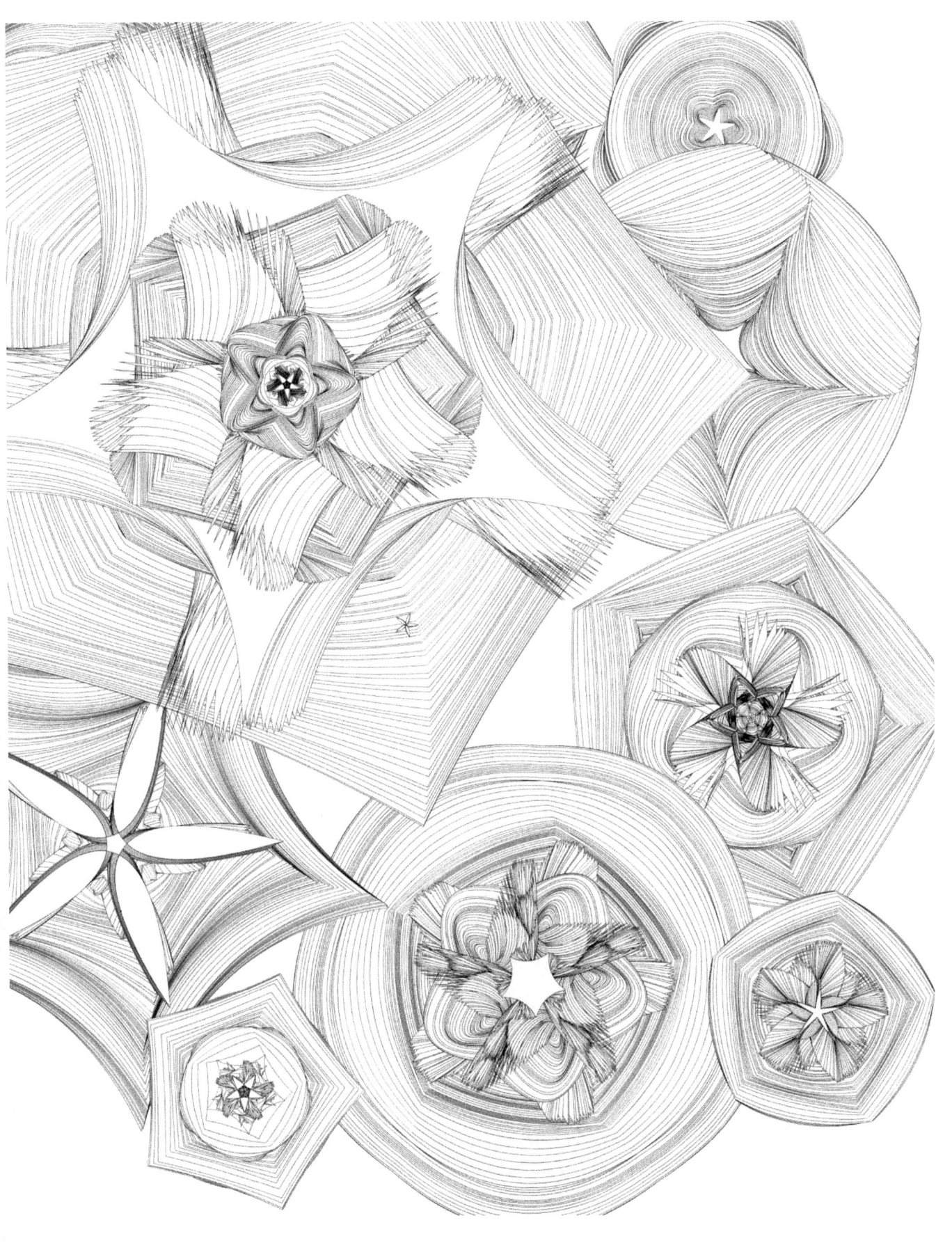

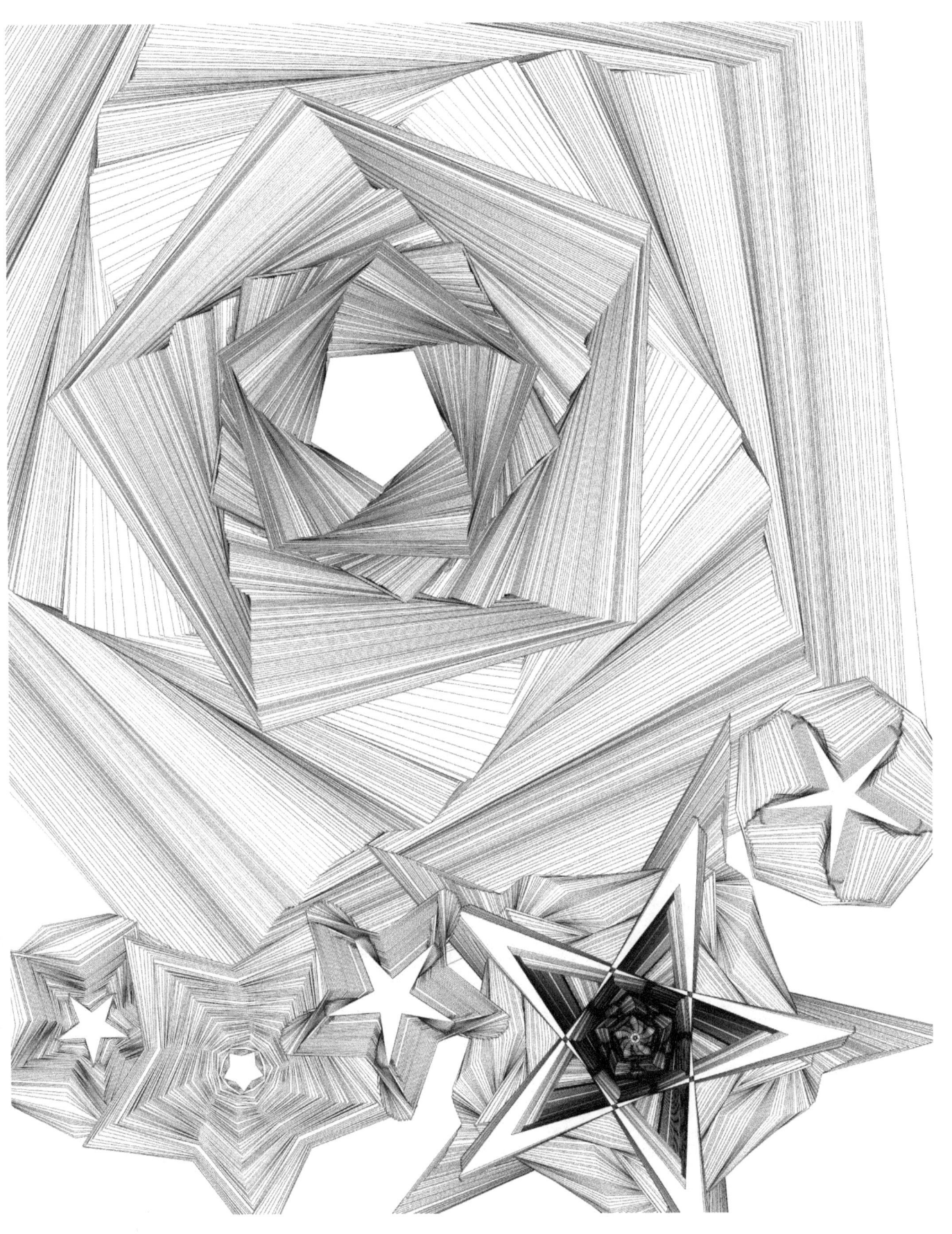

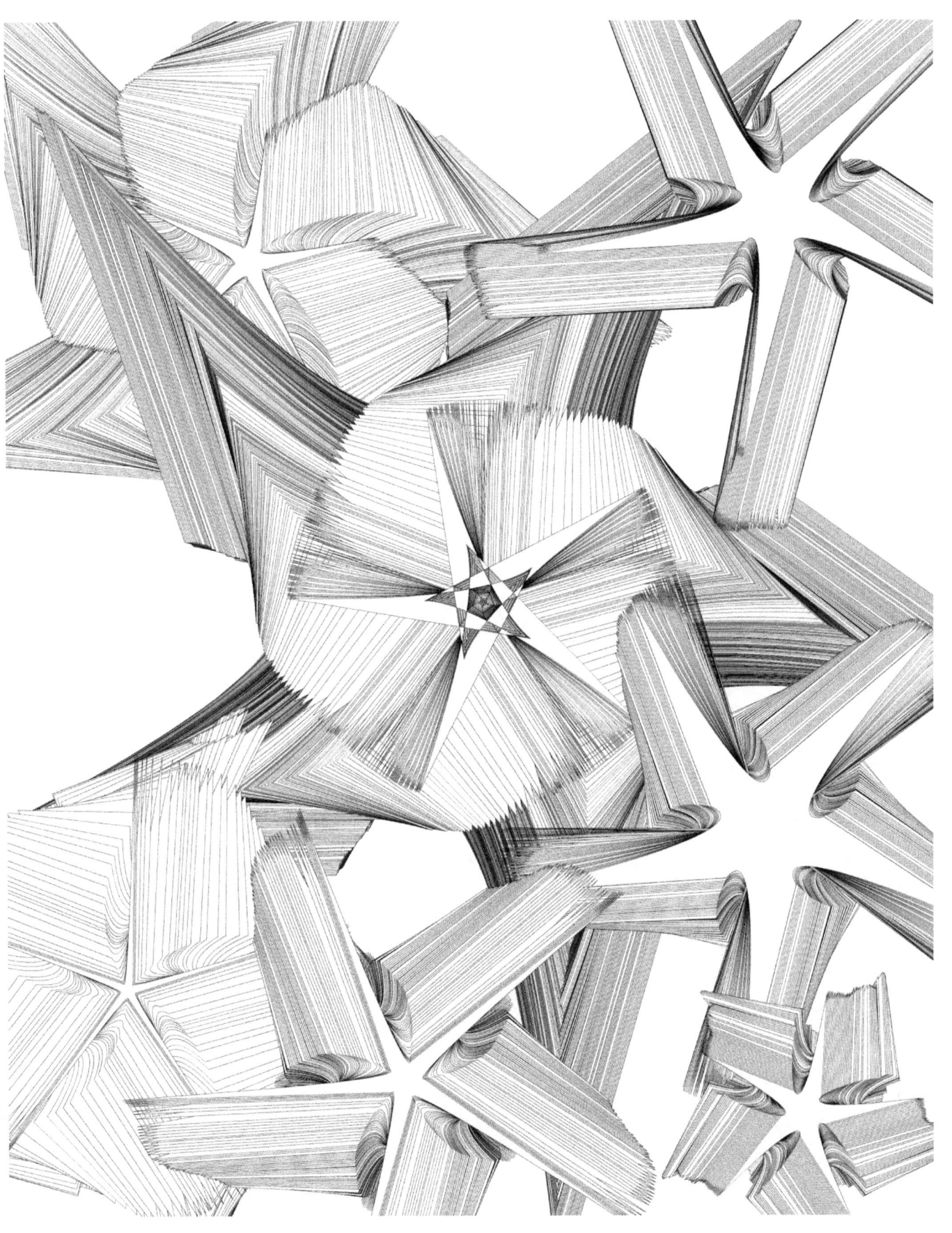

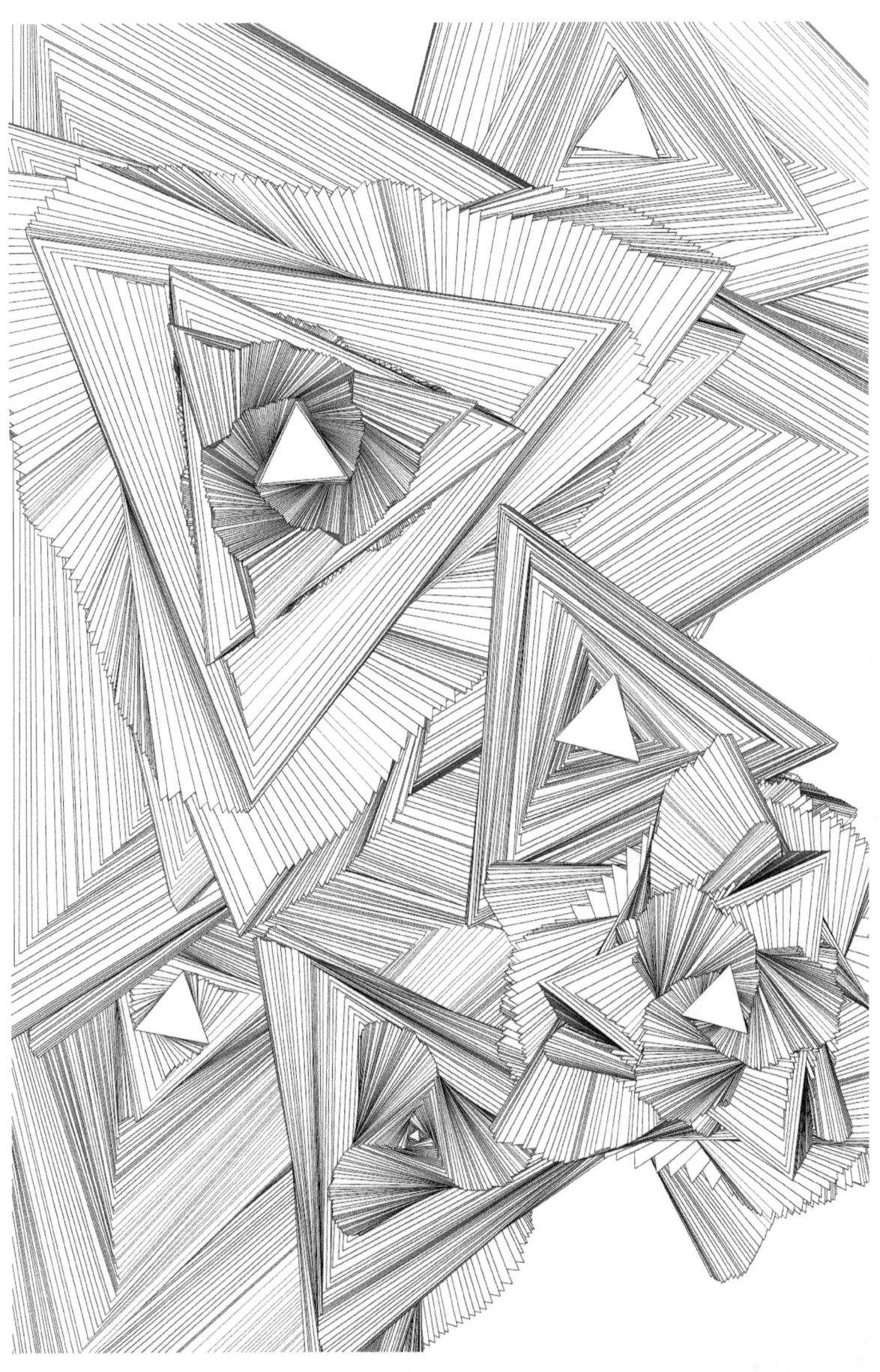